APPLE WATCH SERIES 10 USER GUIDE

A Complete Walkthrough for Setting Up,
Personalizing, and Unlocking Hidden Features for
Everyday Use

ALBERT F. JOHNSON

DISCLAIMER

This guide is an independent publication and is not affiliated with, authorized, sponsored, or endorsed by Apple Inc. "Apple," "Apple Watch," and related terms are trademarks of Apple Inc.

The information provided is for educational and informational purposes only. While every effort has been made to ensure accuracy, the author and publisher make no warranties, express or implied, and are not liable for any damages arising from the use of this guide.

The health features described, including heart rate, blood oxygen, and sleep tracking, are intended for general wellness only and are not substitutes for professional medical advice or diagnosis.

All trademarks and product names are the property of their respective owners.

TABLE OF CONTENT

Introduction

You finally have the Apple Watch Series 10 in your hands—the thinnest, smartest, and most powerful wearable Apple has ever made.

With its sleek new design, ground-breaking health features, and smarter connectivity, it's easy to feel a mix of excitement and uncertainty. Where do you start? How do you make sure you're getting the most out of this incredible device without feeling overwhelmed?

That's exactly why this guide exists—to turn your excitement into complete confidence.

This isn't just another instruction manual. It's your personal companion to mastering the Apple Watch Series 10, step by step. Whether you're unboxing your first smartwatch or upgrading from an older model, this guide is designed to walk you through every feature clearly, simply, and without the tech jargon.

You'll discover how to set up your watch in minutes, personalize it to fit your lifestyle, harness the full power of health and fitness tracking, stay seamlessly connected on the go, and troubleshoot common issues with ease.

By the time you finish, you won't just *use* your Apple Watch—you'll own it like a pro.

No matter your experience level—whether you're a newcomer, a casual user, or a tech enthusiast—this book is made for you. You can move at your own pace, dive deeper into what interests you most, and come back to it whenever you need a quick answer or a new tip.

This guide was created with real questions from real users in mind, making sure every chapter helps you solve problems, unlock features, and enjoy your watch to its fullest potential.

So, get ready. You're about to experience everything your Apple Watch Series 10 was built for—and so much more. **Let's begin.**

Chapter 1

Introduction to Apple Watch Series 10

What's New in Series 10?

The Apple Watch Series 10 marks a bold step forward in the evolution of smartwatches. Thinner, lighter, and with the largest display ever on an Apple Watch, it redefines what wearable technology can feel like. Beyond its elegant redesign, Series 10 introduces powerful new features such as sleep apnea detection, advanced fitness metrics like Training Load, and a new double tap gesture that makes navigating your watch easier than ever—even when your hands are full.

Under the hood, the new S10 chip delivers faster performance with better energy efficiency, ensuring smoother app experiences and longer battery life. Combined with a stunning wide-angle OLED display and new case materials—including the return of premium titanium options—Series 10 isn't just an upgrade; it's a leap.

Whether you're here for the health insights, the fitness tracking, or simply a smarter way to stay connected, the Series 10 offers more than ever before—all packed into a sleeker, more comfortable design.

Key Features at a Glance

- Thinner, Larger Display:
  A noticeably slimmer profile with a 30% larger screen compared to earlier

models, making everything easier to read and interact with.

- **S10 Processor:**
  A powerful, efficient chip that boosts speed, responsiveness, and battery life.

- **Sleep Apnea Detection:**
  Advanced sensors that monitor breathing patterns during sleep to alert you to potential health concerns.

- **Training Load Monitoring:**
  Detailed insights into workout intensity and recovery, helping you train smarter and avoid overexertion.

- **Double Tap Gesture:**
  A new way to control your watch—answer calls, scroll through widgets,

or start activities with just a quick tap of your fingers.

- **Durable, Premium Materials:** Aluminum and titanium case options, with a variety of finishes to match your style.

- **Fast Charging:** Achieves up to 80% battery in about 30 minutes, keeping you ready to move when you need it most.

- **Water Resistance:** Safe for swimming and water activities, with depth and temperature tracking for added adventures.

Who Is This Watch For?

The Apple Watch Series 10 is designed for anyone who wants more from their wrist than just telling time.

- **First-time smartwatch users** will appreciate its easy setup, intuitive navigation, and how seamlessly it integrates with their iPhone.

- **Fitness enthusiasts** will find a trusted companion in its workout tracking, Training Load metrics, and real-time health monitoring.

- **Health-conscious users** can rely on its heart rate alerts, sleep apnea detection, and Emergency SOS features for added peace of mind.

- **Busy professionals and multitaskers** will love the way the watch keeps calls, texts, and reminders at their fingertips—even when their phone is out of reach.

- **Upgraders from older models** will notice a significant jump in comfort, speed, and feature richness, making it a worthy replacement for Series 7, Series 8, and even Series 9 owners.

In short, if you're looking for a smarter, sleeker, and more powerful connection to your daily life—whether at work, at the gym, or on the go—the Apple Watch Series 10 was built for you.

Chapter 2

Getting Started

Compatibility Requirements

Before you begin setting up your Apple Watch Series 10, make sure your devices are ready to work together.

Your iPhone must meet the following requirements:

- iPhone 12 or newer
- Running iOS 18 or later

Why does this matter?

The Series 10 relies heavily on your iPhone for setup, data syncing, and updates. Without the right version of iOS, some features—like Sleep Apnea detection or the new Double Tap gesture—may not work properly.

How to check your iPhone's iOS version:

1. Open the **Settings** app.

2. Tap **General** → **About**.

3. Look at the "iOS Version."

If you need an update:

- Connect your iPhone to Wi-Fi and a charger.

- Go to **Settings** → **General** → **Software Update**, and follow the prompts.

Important Tip:

Backup your iPhone before any major updates. You can do this through iCloud or Finder (Mac) to avoid any data loss.

Unboxing Your Apple Watch Series 10

Unboxing your new Apple Watch is a moment worth savoring.

Inside the box, you'll find:

- The Apple Watch Series 10 (the watch face itself)

- A matching sport band or the band you selected

- Magnetic Fast Charger to USB-C cable

- Basic documentation (Quick Start guide and warranty information)

First steps when unboxing:

- Carefully remove all protective coverings.

- Attach the band by sliding it into the watch grooves until you hear a soft click.

- Adjust the band to fit snugly—but not too tightly—around your wrist.

Band Tips:

- You can swap bands easily without tools.

- Make sure the back sensors touch your skin properly for accurate heart rate and health monitoring.

Packaging Note:

If you ordered an extra band or case, they might arrive in a separate box—this is normal for Apple products.

Charging Your Watch for the First Time

Your Apple Watch comes partially charged, but it's best to top it up fully before setup.

To charge your watch:

1. Plug the USB-C end of the charging cable into a power adapter or powered USB port.

2. Place the magnetic side of the charger against the back of the Apple Watch.

3. You'll feel it snap into place and see a green lightning bolt icon on the screen.

Key Charging Tips:

- **Use an Apple-certified adapter** for best results. (20W recommended for fast charging.)

- **Positioning matters:** Make sure nothing is blocking the magnetic connection.

Charging Time Estimates:

- 0% to 80% in about 30 minutes

- Full charge (100%) in about 60–75 minutes

Battery Calibration Tip:

Allow the first full charge to complete without interruptions. It helps your device more accurately report future battery estimates.

Setting Up and Pairing with Your iPhone

Now comes the exciting part—bringing your Apple Watch to life!

How to pair your watch:

1. Turn on your Apple Watch by pressing and holding the side button until the Apple logo appears.

2. Bring your iPhone close to the watch. A pairing screen should appear automatically on your iPhone.

3. Tap **Continue**, or open the **Apple Watch app** and tap **Start Pairing** manually.

4. Center the watch face in the iPhone's viewfinder when prompted.

5. Choose your setup option:

   o **Set Up as New Watch** (recommended for new users)

- Restore from Backup
  (recommended for upgrading
  users)

6. Follow the onscreen instructions to customize settings:

   - Wrist preference (left or right)

   - Enable Siri

   - Set up a passcode

   - Configure Apple Pay if desired

   - Enable activity tracking and health features

Helpful Tips:

- Keep your iPhone and Apple Watch next to each other during the entire setup process.

- If pairing fails initially, restart both devices and try again.

- Some setup options, like cellular activation, can be skipped and configured later.

Transferring from an Older Apple Watch

Already an Apple Watch user? Good news: Apple makes migration simple and smooth.

Before starting, do this:

- Make sure your old watch is **backed up** to your iPhone (it happens automatically during regular use).

When setting up your Series 10:

- Choose **Restore from Backup** instead of setting up as new.

- Select the most recent backup during setup.

- Wait for your apps, watch faces, settings, and data to transfer.

Special Notes for Upgraders:

- If your old watch had a cellular plan, you'll be prompted to transfer or set up the same plan on your new watch.

- Health and fitness data will migrate automatically if Health syncing is enabled on your iPhone.

Backup Tip:

To ensure a fresh backup, unpair your old watch manually before setting up the new one.

This triggers the iPhone to create a new, up-to-date backup instantly.

Choosing Between GPS and Cellular Models

If you haven't yet finalized your decision, here's a closer look:

Feature	GPS Model	GPS + Cellular Model
Calls and Texts	Via iPhone connection	Independent via carrier plan
Internet Access	Via iPhone Wi-Fi or Bluetooth	Independent using cellular data
Price	Lower	Higher (watch + monthly plan)

Feature	GPS Model	GPS + Cellular Model
Ideal For	Users who always carry their iPhone	Runners, bikers, travelers, people who want freedom from their phone

Key Considerations:

- The Cellular model adds true independence—you can leave your phone at home and still make calls, use Maps, stream music, or send texts.

- However, a monthly carrier fee (typically $10–15/month) applies for standalone cellular use.

- If you rarely leave your phone behind, the GPS-only model is likely enough.

Carrier Setup Tip:

If you choose a Cellular model, check with your mobile carrier first to confirm compatibility and activation steps.

Chapter 3

Navigating Your Apple Watch

Understanding the Home Screen and App Grid

The Home Screen is the central hub of your Apple Watch, where all your apps live.

When you press the **Digital Crown**, you'll be taken to the Home Screen, which displays your apps in one of two styles:

- **Grid View**: Apps are arranged in a honeycomb-like pattern (default).

- **List View**: Apps are displayed in an easy-to-scroll alphabetical list.

How to Switch Views:

1. Press the **Digital Crown** to go to the Home Screen.

2. Firmly press (long-press) anywhere on the Home Screen until options appear.

3. Tap **List View** or **Grid View** based on your preference.

Tips for Navigating the Home Screen:

- In **Grid View**, drag your finger around to move across apps. Tap any app to open it.

- In **List View**, scroll the Digital Crown up or down to browse the list, then tap to open.

- If you ever get lost, simply press the **Digital Crown** once to return to the Watch Face.

Pro Tip:

Organize your apps with the **Watch app** on your iPhone.

Go to **Watch app** → **App Layout** and drag apps to where you want them for quicker access.

Using the Digital Crown and Side Button

Your Apple Watch has two main physical controls:

- **The Digital Crown** (the round dial on the side)

- **The Side Button** (located just below the Crown)

Understanding Their Functions:

Button	Main Actions
Digital Crown	- Press once to return to the Watch Face or open the Home Screen. - Turn to scroll, zoom, or adjust. - Press and hold to activate Siri.
Side Button	- Press once to open the Dock (recent apps). - Press and hold to access Emergency SOS and power options. - Double-click to access Apple Pay quickly.

How to Use Them Together:

- **Screenshot:** Press the Digital Crown and Side Button together quickly to

take a screenshot (enable in Settings →
General → Screenshots).

- **Force Restart:** Press and hold both
  buttons for about 10 seconds if your
  watch becomes unresponsive.

Pro Tip:

Get comfortable turning the Digital Crown
with your fingertip during workouts—it
allows you to adjust volume or scroll
without tapping the screen.

Mastering Gestures: Swipes, Taps, and Double Tap Gesture

Your Apple Watch isn't just about buttons—
it's designed for intuitive gestures.

Basic Gestures You Need to Know:

- **Tap:**

  Lightly tap the screen to select or open items.

- **Swipe:**

  Swipe up, down, left, or right to navigate.

  - Swipe down from the top to view notifications.

  - Swipe up from the bottom to access Control Center.

  - Swipe left or right on the Watch Face to switch faces quickly.

- **Press and Hold (Haptic Touch):** Press and hold the screen to customize Watch Faces or reveal hidden options within apps.

The New Double Tap Gesture (Series 10 Exclusive): One of the most exciting features of the Apple Watch Series 10 is the **Double Tap Gesture**, allowing hands-free control using just your fingers.

How it Works:

- Simply **tap your index finger and thumb together twice.**

- The watch detects the motion and triggers a default action based on the app you're using.

What You Can Do with Double Tap:

- Answer or end calls

- Play or pause music

- Scroll through Smart Stack widgets

- Start a workout or stop a timer

- Snooze alarms

How to Customize Double Tap:

1. Open the **Settings** app on your Apple Watch.

2. Tap **Gestures** → **Double Tap**.

3. Choose your preferred actions where customization is available.

Helpful   Tip:
Practice Double Tapping slowly and deliberately at first. The watch is highly sensitive but may need a slight learning curve for perfect recognition.

Customizing the Control Center

The Control Center is your shortcut panel for quick settings access.

How to Access:

- Swipe **up** from the bottom of the Watch Face to open Control Center.

- (Swipe down if you're already inside an app first.)

Common Controls You'll Find:

- Battery Percentage and Low Power Mode

- Wi-Fi Connection

- Airplane Mode

- Silent Mode

- Flashlight

- Do Not Disturb (Focus Modes)

- Ping iPhone (to locate your phone)

Customizing Your Control Center:

1. Open the Control Center.

2. Scroll to the bottom and tap **Edit**.

3. Drag the icons to rearrange them based on what you use most often.

4. Tap **Done** when finished.

Why Customize It?

- If you frequently use certain settings (like quickly turning on Silent Mode at meetings or activating Water Lock at the pool), moving them to the top saves you precious time.

Pro Tip:

The Ping iPhone feature is a lifesaver when you misplace your iPhone nearby. Tap it once to make your phone emit a sound— even if it's on Silent.

Chapter 4

Personalizing Your Watch

Changing and Customizing Watch Faces

Your Apple Watch Face isn't just about telling time — it's your dashboard for quick information and personal style.

How to Change the Watch Face:

1. Press and hold anywhere on your current Watch Face.

2. Swipe left or right to browse available faces.

3. Tap **New (+)** to add a new face from the gallery.

4. Swipe through the options and tap the one you want.

Customizing a Watch Face:

- After selecting a Watch Face, tap **Edit**.

- You'll see different customization areas:

  - **Style/Color**: Adjust the overall look.

  - **Complications**: Add useful widgets like Weather, Calendar, or Activity Rings.

Helpful Tip:

Many faces have different themes—try Modular, Infograph, or Portraits to match your needs.

You can even create multiple versions of a face (for example: one for work, one for workouts).

Adding, Moving, and Removing Apps

You can install apps directly onto your Apple Watch, giving you instant access to workouts, music, reminders, and more.

Adding Apps:

- On your **iPhone**:

    1. Open the **Watch** app.

    2. Tap the **App Store** tab.

    3. Browse or search for apps, then tap **Get** or **Download**.

- Directly on your **Apple Watch**:

    1. Open the **App Store** app.

    2. Browse, tap, and download apps just like on your iPhone.

Moving Apps:

- Press the Digital Crown to open the Home Screen.

- If using **Grid View:**

  - Press and hold any app icon until they start to jiggle.

  - Drag an app to a new spot.

  - Press the Digital Crown again to save the layout.

Removing Apps:

- Press and hold an app until it jiggles.

- Tap the small **X** that appears on the app icon.

- Confirm deletion if prompted.

Note:

Deleting an app from your watch usually does not remove it from your iPhone.

Pro Tip:

Keep only your most-used apps on your Watch to free up space and simplify navigation.

Setting Up Complications for Quick Access

Complications are mini-widgets that display information or quick shortcuts right on your Watch Face — like battery life, next appointment, weather, or workout start buttons.

How to Add or Edit Complications:

1. Press and hold your Watch Face → Tap **Edit**.

2. Swipe left until you reach the **Complications** screen.

3. Tap a complication area and choose what you want to display.

Types of Useful Complications:

- Calendar (upcoming meetings)

- Workout shortcut

- Weather

- Heart Rate monitor

- Activity Rings

- Music controls

Helpful Tip:

Some Watch Faces allow more complications than others.

Infograph Modular and **Wayfinder** (on

Cellular models) offer many complication slots if you love quick access tools.

Adjusting Settings: Display, Sounds, and Haptics

Make your Apple Watch truly yours by adjusting basic settings for comfort and functionality.

Display Settings:

- Brightness:

  - Open **Settings** → **Display & Brightness** → Adjust brightness slider.

- **Always-On Display** (Series 10 models support it):

  - Toggle Always-On Display to conserve battery if needed.

- Text Size and Bold Text:

    o Adjust for easier reading under Settings → **Display & Brightness** → **Text Size.**

Sounds and Haptics:

- Volume Control:

    o Settings → **Sounds & Haptics** → Adjust the alert volume slider.

- Haptic Alerts:

    o Turn on **Prominent Haptic** for stronger vibration feedback (good if you often miss notifications).

Helpful Tip:

If you don't want to disturb others (e.g., in meetings), quickly activate **Silent Mode** by swiping up for Control Center and tapping the Bell icon.

Setting Up Apple Pay on Your Watch

Apple Pay on your watch lets you tap and pay at stores, vending machines, and public transport without touching your phone or wallet.

To Set Up Apple Pay:

1. Open the **Watch app** on your iPhone.

2. Tap **Wallet & Apple Pay**.

3. Tap **Add Card**.

4. Follow the instructions to add a debit or credit card (you may need to verify it with your bank).

Using Apple Pay:

- Double-click the **Side Button** on your Apple Watch.

- Your default card will appear.

- Hold the watch face near the payment terminal.

- A gentle tap and beep confirm your payment.

Helpful Tip:

You can add multiple cards and switch between them quickly during checkout by swiping on the screen before tapping.

Chapter 5

Staying Connected

Making and Receiving Calls

One of the biggest advantages of the Apple Watch Series 10 is staying reachable even when your iPhone isn't in hand.

How to Make a Call:

- Using the Phone App:

    1. Press the Digital Crown to open the app list.

    2. Tap the **Phone** app.

    3. Select **Contacts**, **Keypad**, or **Recents**.

    4. Tap a contact or dial a number to call.

- Using Siri:

  o Raise your wrist and say, "Call [Contact Name]."

- Using Favorites:

  o Add contacts to Favorites (through the Phone app on your iPhone) for quicker access.

How to Receive a Call:

- When a call comes in, your Apple Watch vibrates and displays caller info.

- **Answer:** Tap the green phone icon.

- **Decline:** Tap the red phone icon.

Audio Tips:

- **Speakerphone:** Default call audio comes through the Watch's built-in speaker.

- **Bluetooth Earbuds:** If paired with AirPods or other Bluetooth headphones, the call audio automatically routes there.

- **Clear Calls:** Thanks to upgraded microphones and noise suppression in Series 10, call clarity is noticeably better—even outdoors.

Sending Messages and Emails

You can easily send quick replies, dictate messages, or use pre-written responses.

Sending Messages:

- Using the Messages App:

  1. Open the **Messages** app.

  2. Tap an existing conversation or tap **New Message**.

3. Choose a contact, then dictate your message, use Scribble, or pick a preset reply.

- Using Siri:
  - Raise your wrist and say, "Text [Contact Name]: [Your Message]."

Replying to Messages:

- Tap on a received message.

- Choose how you want to reply:
  - Dictation (Speak your message)
  - Scribble (Draw letters)
  - Emoji
  - Prewritten quick replies (like "OK," "Thanks!")

Sending Emails:

- Open the **Mail** app to check emails.

- Tap **Compose** to dictate or respond to emails.

- Email typing is simplified; dictation works best for longer replies.

Pro Tip:

You can customize quick replies in the Watch app under **Messages → Default Replies** for more personalized responses.

Using Siri on Your Apple Watch

Siri is smarter and more integrated than ever on the Apple Watch Series 10, letting you stay hands-free.

Ways to Activate Siri:

- **Raise to Speak:** Simply raise your wrist and start talking—no "Hey Siri" needed.

- **Digital Crown:** Press and hold the Digital Crown until Siri appears.

- **Voice Command:** Say "Hey Siri" (if enabled).

What You Can Ask Siri:

- Send messages and make calls

- Set timers, alarms, and reminders

- Ask for weather updates

- Control smart home devices

- Start workouts or music

- Search the web (simple queries only)

Helpful Tip:

If Siri doesn't respond immediately, check that "Raise to Speak" and "Hey Siri" are both enabled in **Settings** → **Siri** on your Watch.

Fact from Research:

Many users find Raise-to-Speak on the Series 10 more responsive compared to earlier models, thanks to the updated S10 processor.

Managing Notifications Effectively

Notifications on your wrist can be incredibly convenient—or overwhelming if unmanaged.

Viewing Notifications:

- Swipe **down** from the top of the Watch Face to see missed notifications.

Customizing Notifications:

- Open the **Watch app** on your iPhone.

- Tap **Notifications**.

- Choose how you want each app to notify you:

- Mirror iPhone alerts

- Customize separately for the Watch

- Turn off notifications for specific apps entirely

Notification Best Practices:

- Only allow notifications from important apps like Messages, Calendar, and Workouts.

- Turn off notifications for low-priority apps (games, non-essential updates) to avoid constant buzzing.

- Use **Focus Modes** to control notifications during workouts, work hours, or sleep.

Helpful Tip:

On the Watch itself, you can quickly mute notifications for an app by swiping left on a notification and tapping **Options → Mute**.

Fact from Research:

Real-world users love that Series 10's haptics make notifications subtle but easy to notice — they no longer miss important alerts even without sound.

Using Cellular Connectivity Without Your iPhone

If you have the **GPS + Cellular** model, you can stay connected even without your iPhone nearby—perfect for runners, bikers, or people who want to stay light.

How Cellular Connectivity Works:

- Your Apple Watch uses its built-in LTE radio to connect directly to your carrier network.

- You can call, text, stream music, check maps, and use apps that need data independently.

Setting Up Cellular:

- During Watch setup, you'll be asked if you want to add a plan.

- If skipped, you can later go to:

  - **iPhone Watch app → Cellular → Set Up Cellular.**

- Follow your carrier's instructions (may involve extra monthly charges).

Checking Connection:

- On the Watch Face or Control Center, a green or white cellular icon shows connection strength.

  - **Green dots** mean connected directly to the carrier.

  - **White dots** mean connected over Wi-Fi or Bluetooth.

Battery Caution:

Using cellular heavily (calls, streaming music, navigation) can drain your battery faster than using the Watch connected to your iPhone.

Helpful Tip:

When you're on cellular, use lightweight apps (like Messages or simple music playlists) to preserve battery if you'll be out for a long time.

Fact from Research:

Many users reported that Series 10's cellular performance is stronger and more stable than older models, making it a true replacement for light smartphone use when out and about.

Chapter 6

Health and Fitness Tracking

Setting Up and Using the Activity Rings

The Apple Watch Series 10 turns fitness into a daily goal with its three Activity Rings:

Ring	Meaning
Move (Red)	Tracks active calories burned.
Exercise (Green)	Measures minutes of brisk activity.
Stand (Blue)	Tracks how often you stand and move each hour.

Setting Up Activity:

- Open the **Activity** app on your Apple Watch.

- Follow the prompts to set your Move goal (calories), Exercise goal (minutes), and Stand goal (hours).

- You can adjust goals anytime by firmly pressing on the Activity Rings screen and tapping **Change Move Goal**, **Change Exercise Goal**, or **Change Stand Goal**.

How to Use It Daily:

- Check your rings by opening the Activity app.

- Get gentle reminders throughout the day to stand, move, and exercise.

Motivation Tip:

Earn awards for meeting your goals, completing streaks, and achieving personal bests.

Many users find it surprisingly motivating to close all three rings daily!

Tracking Workouts and Exercise Sessions

Your Apple Watch is an excellent workout companion, with specialized modes for nearly every type of exercise.

Starting a Workout:

- Open the **Workout** app.

- Scroll and tap the type of workout (Outdoor Walk, Cycling, Swimming, Yoga, HIIT, etc.).

- Tap to begin.

- Adjust goal metrics (calories, distance, time) if desired.

During a Workout:

- Raise your wrist to view real-time stats like heart rate, calories burned, pace, and distance.

- Pause or end workouts with a swipe or a press of the Digital Crown + Side Button together.

New with Series 10:

- **Training Load:** Tracks workout intensity over time to help you understand strain and recovery needs—ideal for athletes and serious fitness users.

Helpful Tip:

Forgot to start a workout?

The Apple Watch can automatically detect some activities (like walking, running, or swimming) and suggest starting a session mid-activity.

Understanding Heart Rate Monitoring

Heart rate monitoring is at the core of many Apple Watch health features.

How It Works:

- Your watch uses an optical heart sensor (with green LEDs and infrared lights) to detect blood flow and measure your beats per minute (BPM).

- It checks periodically throughout the day and provides detailed graphs in the Health app.

Viewing Heart Rate:

- Open the **Heart Rate** app.

- See your current heart rate, resting heart rate, walking average, and workout heart rates.

Alerts You Can Set:

- **High Heart Rate Alert** (if BPM is abnormally high while inactive).

- **Low Heart Rate Alert** (if BPM drops unusually low).

- **Irregular Rhythm Notification** (may suggest signs of atrial fibrillation).

Fact from Research:

Series 10's heart rate monitoring is even more accurate during intense workouts, thanks to improved sensor design and better skin contact from the thinner watch body.

Using Blood Oxygen Measurements

Series 10 also features a Blood Oxygen sensor, providing insights into your overall wellness.

How to Use It:

- Open the **Blood Oxygen** app.

- Stay still and flat for about 15 seconds during the scan.

- Your SpO_2 percentage appears on-screen (normal levels are generally between 95%–100%).

Background Measurements:

- Blood Oxygen levels are automatically monitored periodically in the background (especially during sleep) if enabled.

Helpful Tip:

Wearing the watch snugly and keeping it clean helps ensure more accurate blood oxygen readings.

Important Note:

While helpful, blood oxygen measurements are not a medical diagnostic tool. They provide general wellness insights but do not replace professional medical advice.

Tracking Sleep and Using Sleep Apnea Alerts

Sleep tracking on the Series 10 has become much smarter—and more health-focused.

How to Set Up Sleep Tracking:

1. Open the **Health** app on your iPhone.

2. Tap **Sleep** → **Set Up Sleep**.

3. Set your sleep goal, bedtime, and wake-up time.

4. Enable **Sleep Focus** at night to minimize distractions.

What Sleep Tracking Measures:

- Time spent asleep

- Sleep stages (Deep, REM, Core sleep)

- Heart rate during sleep

- Blood oxygen levels during sleep (if enabled)

Sleep Apnea Detection (New in Series 10):

- The watch monitors breathing interruptions and patterns.

- If potential sleep apnea symptoms are detected, it can recommend you seek further evaluation.

Fact from Research:

Many users report that Sleep Apnea alerts are subtle but valuable, providing early warnings about possible breathing disturbances during sleep.

Setting Up Emergency SOS and Fall Detection

Your Apple Watch isn't just a fitness tracker—it's a lifesaver.

Emergency SOS Setup:

- Press and hold the **Side Button** until the Emergency SOS slider appears.

- Slide to call emergency services, or continue holding to auto-call if enabled.

- Emergency contacts will also be notified automatically.

Fall Detection Setup:

- Open the **Watch** app on your iPhone.

- Tap **Emergency SOS**.

- Toggle **Fall Detection** ON.

How Fall Detection Works:

- If your watch detects a hard fall, it taps your wrist, sounds an alarm, and displays an alert.

- If you're unresponsive after about a minute, it automatically calls emergency services.

Helpful Tip:

Fall Detection is especially helpful for older adults, athletes, and anyone working in risky environments.

Fact from Research:

Series 10 has even improved fall detection algorithms, making it more accurate in distinguishing between real falls and minor stumbles compared to previous models.

Chapter 7

Apps and Media

Installing Apps from the App Store

Your Apple Watch Series 10 isn't limited to the apps it comes with—you can expand its abilities by downloading apps directly from the App Store.

How to Install Apps:

- On Your Watch:

    1. Press the Digital Crown to open the Home Screen.

    2. Find and tap the **App Store**.

    3. Use Scribble, dictation, or the keyboard to search for an app.

4. Tap **Get** or the price button to download.

- **On Your iPhone:**

  1. Open the **Watch** app.

  2. Tap the **App Store** tab or scroll down to see available apps.

  3. Tap **Install** next to the apps you want.

Helpful Tips:

- Some iPhone apps automatically have companion Watch apps (e.g., Spotify, Nike Run Club, Audible).

- You can turn off **Automatic App Install** if you prefer to manually control what's on your Watch (**Watch app** → **General** → **Automatic App Install**).

Fact from Research:

Series 10 users appreciate that the updated App Store interface is faster and smoother than before, making direct-from-watch installs more convenient.

Listening to Music, Podcasts, and Audiobooks

Your Apple Watch lets you take your favorite entertainment anywhere—even without your phone.

Listening to Music:

- **Stream:**

  If you have Wi-Fi or Cellular, you can stream Apple Music or Spotify directly.

- **Download:**

  1. Open the **Watch app** on your iPhone.

2. Tap **Music** → **Add Music**.

3. Select albums, playlists, or artists to sync to your watch.

Listening to Podcasts:

- Apple's Podcast app can stream or download episodes for offline listening.

- Spotify and Audible also allow podcast playback through their apps.

Listening to Audiobooks:

- Sync audiobooks from your iPhone's **Books** app.

- Go to the Watch app → **Audiobooks** → **Add Audiobooks**.

Helpful Tip:

Always pair Bluetooth headphones (like AirPods) to listen on the go.

Go to **Settings** → **Bluetooth** → **Pair Device** on your Watch.

Fact from Research:

Series 10's faster processor means less lag when streaming or downloading media— many users noticed smoother transitions and faster buffering, especially for offline playlists.

Using Maps, Calendar, and Reminders

Your Watch can guide your day just as much as your iPhone can—if not more conveniently.

Maps on Apple Watch:

- Open the **Maps** app to search or view directions.

- Get **Turn-by-Turn Navigation** directly on your wrist, with haptic taps signaling upcoming turns.

- Great for walking directions in cities or biking routes.

Using Calendar:

- View your upcoming events, invitations, and schedules.

- Tap an event for more details.

- Use Siri to add events quickly: "Hey Siri, schedule a meeting for tomorrow at 10 AM."

Setting Reminders:

- Open the **Reminders** app.

- Tap **New Reminder**.

- Add a title, time, and location if needed.

- Siri makes this even faster: "Remind me to call Mom at 6 PM."

Helpful Tip:

Using Location-Based Reminders (e.g., "Remind me to grab groceries when I leave work") works perfectly with the GPS on your Watch when paired to your iPhone or active over Cellular.

Using Camera Remote and Other Built-in Tools

Even without a big screen, the Apple Watch offers smart tools you'll use every day.

Camera Remote:

- Open the **Camera Remote** app on your Watch.

- It automatically connects to your iPhone's camera.

- You can:

  - See a live preview

  - Tap to focus

  - Adjust settings like timer or flash

  - Tap the Shutter button on the Watch to take a photo

- Perfect for group selfies, tripod shots, or stable videos!

Other Built-in Tools:

- **Weather App:** Check real-time weather forecasts and upcoming conditions.

- **Timer, Stopwatch, Alarm:** Quickly start or customize timers and alarms right from your wrist.

- **Voice Memos:** Record quick audio notes—ideal during meetings or while exercising.

- **Find My Devices:** Ping your iPhone, locate AirTags, and even find friends with the Find People app.

Helpful Tip:

The Camera Remote works even from 30–40 feet away, depending on your surroundings. Great for outdoor photoshoots or family portraits.

Fact from Research:

Real-world users say Camera Remote and Find My iPhone are among the most-loved "small" features they use almost daily—especially busy professionals and travelers.

Chapter 8

Battery Life and Charging

Battery Life Expectations

The Apple Watch Series 10 brings improvements in both performance and efficiency, but it's important to know what you can realistically expect when it comes to battery life.

Typical Battery Life:

- Up to **18 hours** of standard usage on a full charge.

- Includes activities like notifications, app usage, GPS workouts, music playback, and occasional calls.

With Low Power Mode:

- You can extend usage up to **36 hours** by limiting background activity and screen refreshes.

Real-World Tip:

Battery life can vary based on usage— intense workouts, extended GPS tracking, cellular use without iPhone nearby, or heavy app usage (like streaming media) will drain the battery faster.

Fact from Research:

Series 10 users noticed that even with more features packed in, overall battery endurance is slightly better than Series 9 during moderate day-to-day use, especially with smarter app background refreshing.

Tips to Extend Battery Life

If you want to stretch your battery life further—especially during long days, travel, or workouts—these tips help:

Optimize Screen Settings:

- Lower screen brightness:

    ○ Settings → Display & Brightness → Adjust Brightness.

- Reduce Always-On Display usage:

    ○ Settings → Display & Brightness → Always On → Toggle Off (if you don't mind lifting your wrist).

Control Background Activity:

- Limit background app refresh:

- Watch app on iPhone → General → Background App Refresh → Turn off for non-essential apps.

Manage Notifications:

- Turn off non-critical notifications that wake the screen frequently (Settings → Notifications).

Disable Unused Features:

- Turn off Wi-Fi or Cellular when not needed (Control Center).

- Disable Wake on Wrist Raise if unnecessary (Settings → General → Wake Screen).

Workout Power Savings:

- In longer workout sessions, consider enabling Low Power Mode to cut down on heart rate sampling and GPS usage when not critical.

Helpful Tip:

Adding a shortcut for Low Power Mode to your Control Center makes it quick to toggle when you need it.

Using Low Power Mode

Low Power Mode is a brilliant tool for getting the most from your Watch when battery life becomes a priority.

What Low Power Mode Does:

- Reduces display brightness and refresh rate

- Pauses background app refresh

- Limits heart rate measurements (only occasional readings during workouts)

- Turns off Always-On Display

How to Enable It:

- Open **Control Center** (Swipe Up).

- Tap the battery percentage.

- Toggle **Low Power Mode** ON.

You can also schedule Low Power Mode automatically:

- Settings → Battery → Low Power Mode → Enable during workouts or at specific battery levels.

Real-World Example:

Many users toggle Low Power Mode when attending long events (weddings, conferences) where charging isn't convenient, easily pushing a full day's use without worry.

Helpful Tip:

Low Power Mode still allows basic calling, messaging, and fitness tracking—you'll just lose some background syncing temporarily.

Fast Charging Basics

Fast charging is a key strength of the Apple Watch Series 10, especially when you're in a hurry.

What You Need:

- The included **Apple USB-C Magnetic Fast Charging Cable.**

- A **20W or higher USB-C Power Adapter** (sold separately if not included).

Fast Charging Performance:

- **0% to 80% charge in about 30 minutes.**

- Full 100% charge usually takes about 60–75 minutes.

Helpful Tips for Fast Charging:

- Place the watch perfectly flat on the charger — misalignment can slow charging.

- If possible, avoid charging in extremely hot environments (heat can slow down or protectively pause fast charging).

- For the quickest boost, use the original or an MFi-certified Apple fast charger rather than third-party cables.

Fact from Research:

Real users love that a short charge while showering or getting ready in the morning often gives enough battery for an entire day—making daily battery anxiety a thing of the past.

Chapter 9

Advanced Tips and Tricks

Using Theater Mode, Silent Mode, and Water Lock

The Apple Watch Series 10 offers smart quick-access modes to help you manage different environments—whether you're in a movie theater, attending a meeting, or jumping into the pool.

Theater Mode:

- **Purpose:** Prevents the display from waking when you raise your wrist and silences notifications.

- **When to Use:** Movie theaters, concerts, religious services, meetings, anywhere you don't want your watch lighting up.

- **How to Enable:**

    - Swipe up from the Watch Face to open **Control Center**.

    - Tap the **Theater Masks** icon (two faces).

- **Helpful Tip:**

    Even in Theater Mode, you'll still feel silent haptic taps for notifications— you just won't be disturbed by screen lighting or sounds.

Silent Mode:

- **Purpose:** Silences all audible alerts and system sounds.

- **When to Use:** Meetings, quiet environments, classrooms.

- **How to Enable:**

  - Swipe up for **Control Center**.

  - Tap the **Bell** icon.

- **Helpful Tip:**
  Silent Mode only silences sounds—it doesn't mute haptic feedback. You'll still feel vibrations for calls and notifications.

Water Lock:

- **Purpose:** Locks the screen to prevent accidental touches when exposed to water and helps expel water from the speaker afterward.

- **When to Use:** Swimming, showering, rainy runs.

- **How to Enable:**

  - Open **Control Center**.

  - Tap the **Water Drop** icon.

- After swimming or exposure to water, **turn the Digital Crown** to unlock the screen and expel any water trapped in the speaker.

Fact from Research:

Real-world users have praised Water Lock's usefulness during swimming and even sweaty workouts—it prevents accidental taps and protects your speaker.

Managing Background App Refresh

Background App Refresh can subtly drain your battery and data if not managed well, especially for apps you rarely use.

What Background App Refresh Does:

- Allows apps to update their content in the background so they're ready when you open them.

How to Manage It:

- Open the **Watch app** on your iPhone.

- Go to **General** → **Background App Refresh**.

- Turn off Background Refresh for apps that don't need constant updates (like shopping apps, games, or news feeds).

Helpful Tip:

Keep it ON for critical apps (like Weather, Calendar, Messages) but OFF for less essential apps to maximize battery life and reduce unnecessary data usage.

Fact from Research:

Experienced Series 10 users who actively manage background refresh report noticeably better daily battery performance without losing important functionality.

Using Focus Modes on Apple Watch

Focus Modes let you filter notifications and customize which alerts come through during different activities—directly from your wrist.

Available Focus Modes:

- **Do Not Disturb:** Silences almost everything except alarms.

- **Work Focus:** Allows only work-related notifications.

- **Sleep Focus:** Mutes all non-critical alerts during sleep.

- **Fitness Focus:** Silences non-essential notifications during workouts.

How to Activate Focus Modes:

- Swipe up for **Control Center**.

- Tap the **Crescent Moon** or **Focus** icon.

- Choose the Focus mode you want, or create a custom one through your iPhone's Focus settings.

Smart Activation:

- Focus Modes can be automated based on time, location, or app usage.

- Example: Automatically activate Work Focus when you arrive at the office.

Helpful Tip:

Sync your Focus settings across your Apple devices (iPhone, Mac, iPad) for a seamless, distraction-free experience everywhere.

Fact from Research:

Series 10 owners who consistently use Focus Modes report higher productivity and fewer distractions—especially during workouts, meetings, or personal downtime.

Tracking Medications and Health Data

Series 10 isn't just about fitness—it also helps you stay on top of your health routines, including medications and vital signs.

Setting Up Medication Tracking:

- Open the **Health** app on your iPhone.

- Tap **Browse** → **Medications** → **Add Medication.**

- Enter dosage, frequency, and optional alerts.

How It Works on Your Watch:

- You'll receive discreet reminders when it's time to take your medication.

- Mark medications as taken directly from a notification on your Watch.

Other Health Data to Monitor:

- Heart rate trends

- Blood oxygen levels

- Sleep metrics

- Respiratory rate during sleep

- Activity and fitness history

Helpful Tip:

You can log medications manually if you miss a reminder, ensuring your health records stay accurate.

Fact from Research:

Users who use medication tracking on Series 10 find it incredibly helpful for staying consistent—especially those managing multiple daily prescriptions.

Chapter 10

Troubleshooting Common Issues

If Your Watch Won't Pair or Connect

Sometimes, your Apple Watch Series 10 might refuse to pair with your iPhone—or suddenly lose connection. Don't panic; most issues have simple fixes.

First Steps to Try:

- **Check Bluetooth and Wi-Fi:**

    o Make sure Bluetooth is turned ON on your iPhone (Settings → Bluetooth).

- Ensure both devices are connected to a strong Wi-Fi or Cellular network.

- **Bring Devices Closer:**

  - Keep your iPhone and Watch within a few inches during pairing or reconnecting.

- **Restart Both Devices:**

  - Restart your iPhone and your Watch. Often this clears temporary glitches.

If Still Not Pairing:

- Open the **Watch app** on iPhone → Tap **Start Pairing**.

- If your Watch shows the wrong pairing screen, tap the small "i" icon and manually connect.

Helpful Tip:

Ensure your iPhone is updated to the latest iOS version. Outdated software can block Watch pairing.

Fact from Research:

Real users found that restarting both devices solves pairing problems in more than 70% of cases—before needing more drastic steps.

Fixing Battery Drain Problems

Is your battery dying faster than you expected? A few small adjustments can usually restore normal battery performance.

Common Causes of Fast Drain:

- Background App Refresh left ON for many apps

- Always-On Display brightness too high

- Too many active notifications

- Cellular or GPS use without Wi-Fi connection

- New updates still "settling" after installation

How to Fix It:

- **Update Software:**
  Apple often releases WatchOS updates with battery improvements.

- **Check Battery Usage:**
  Settings → Battery → Review which apps use the most power.

- **Optimize Settings:**

- Lower screen brightness.

- Turn off background refresh for non-essential apps.

- Reduce haptic feedback if not needed.

- Use Low Power Mode during long days or workouts.

Helpful Tip:

After a major update or restoring from backup, battery life might seem worse temporarily—it usually stabilizes within 24–48 hours.

When Notifications Stop Coming In

If your Watch suddenly stops buzzing or showing notifications, it can usually be fixed quickly.

Steps to Troubleshoot:

- **Ensure Watch Is Unlocked and On Wrist:**
  If your Watch is locked or not on your wrist properly, it may block notifications.

- **Check Connection to iPhone:**
  Make sure the Watch is still connected (green phone icon on Watch Face).

- **Check Notification Settings:**
  - Open Watch app on iPhone → Notifications.
  - Make sure the desired apps are allowed to send notifications.

- **Disable Do Not Disturb or Focus Modes:**

Sometimes Focus Modes (Work, Sleep) can silence alerts if left on accidentally.

Helpful Tip:

Restart both your Watch and iPhone if settings seem fine but notifications still don't appear.

Fact from Research:

Many users find that toggling Bluetooth OFF and ON again on the iPhone refreshes the Watch's connection and brings back missing notifications.

Audio and Call Quality Issues

If calls sound distorted, quiet, or robotic on your Watch, there are several fixes to try.

Common Causes:

- Dirty or obstructed speaker grill

- Bluetooth interference

- Poor Wi-Fi or Cellular signal strength

How to Improve Call Quality:

- **Clean the Watch:**
  Gently wipe the speaker area with a soft, dry cloth.
  Water Lock feature helps expel moisture if the Watch was exposed to water.

- **Move to Better Signal Area:**
  Stronger Wi-Fi or Cellular signal dramatically improves call clarity.

- **Restart Watch:**
  Temporary glitches are often cleared by restarting the device.

Helpful Tip:

If you're using AirPods with your Watch and

experiencing laggy audio, unpairing and repairing them often fixes the problem.

Fact from Research:

Users report that Series 10's microphones have noticeably improved voice pickup over Series 8 or Series 9, especially outdoors—but network quality still plays a big role.

Resetting Your Apple Watch

Sometimes, a full reset is the fastest solution—especially if all else fails.

Two Types of Reset:

Reset Type	When to Use	How to Perform
Restart	Minor glitches (not pairing,	Press and hold Side Button → Slide to Power

Reset Type	When to Use	How to Perform
	slow app response)	Off → Turn on again
Erase and Reset	Persistent issues, selling Watch, full software clean-up	Settings → General → Reset → Erase All Content and Settings

Important Notes Before Erasing:

- Backup your Watch data first (automatic with iPhone if paired).

- Unpairing the Watch from your iPhone automatically triggers a fresh backup.

Helpful Tip:

Resetting and restoring from a clean backup solves

many "strange behavior" issues and restores optimal performance.

Chapter 11

Buying Advice and Upgrades

Should You Upgrade to Series 10?

Deciding whether to upgrade depends on what you currently own—and what you expect from your Apple Watch.

Upgrade is Highly Recommended If You Have:

- Series 7 or earlier:
  You'll notice a big difference in speed (thanks to the S10 chip), display size, battery management, and new features like Sleep Apnea Detection and Double Tap Gesture.

115 | P a g e

- A First-Generation SE or Series 3-5:
  The improvements in health tracking, emergency features, and performance make Series 10 a major leap forward.

Upgrade Might Be Optional If You Have:

- Series 8 or Series 9:
  The jump is more evolutionary. You'll still gain a bigger display, a thinner and lighter build, more powerful chip, and the convenience of Double Tap—but if your current Watch works perfectly, you might wait another generation unless you want the latest health tracking upgrades now.

Helpful Tip:

If health insights like advanced sleep apnea monitoring or Training Load tracking are important to you, upgrading to Series 10 makes a clear difference.

Comparing Series 10 vs. Series 9 and Ultra 2

Choosing between the Series 10, Series 9, and the more rugged Ultra 2 depends on your lifestyle needs.

Feature	Series 9	Series 10	Ultra 2
Display	Bright, smaller	Largest, edge-to-edge	Largest, brightest
Body	Slightly thicker	Thinner, lighter	Bulky, rugged
Battery Life	Up to 18 hrs	Up to 18–36 hrs	Up to 36–72 hrs
New Features	Double Tap, basic fitness tracking	Double Tap + Sleep Apnea detection + Training Load	Same features, plus deep-dive outdoor functions (Depth Gauge, Dive Computer)

Summary:

- **Choose Series 10** if you want cutting-edge features in a sleek, everyday wearable.

- **Choose Ultra 2** if you need extreme durability, longer battery life, and specialized adventure features (diving, hiking, etc.).

Fact from Research:

Most casual users and fitness enthusiasts find Series 10 to be the perfect blend of technology and practicality—without the extra bulk of the Ultra models.

Choosing the Right Size and Material

Series 10 comes in two sizes:

- **42mm** and **46mm** case options.

Which Size to Choose:

- **42mm:**

  Ideal for smaller wrists, a lighter and more discreet feel.

- **46mm:**

  Better for larger wrists, people who want maximum screen visibility, or prefer a bolder watch presence.

Material Options:

- **Aluminum:**

  - Lightweight, affordable, perfect for casual users.

  - Comes in colors like Silver, Starlight, Midnight, Pink, and Product(RED).

- **Titanium:**

- More durable, scratch-resistant, and has a premium finish.
- Available in Natural, Black Titanium, and Gold.

Helpful Tip:

If you plan to be very active outdoors or prefer a slightly more luxurious look, Titanium is worth considering for its durability without excessive weight.

Fact from Research:

Titanium Series 10 models feel noticeably lighter and stronger than older stainless steel models, which many upgraders appreciate for daily wear.

Understanding AppleCare+ for Your Watch

AppleCare+ offers additional peace of mind for your investment.

What AppleCare+ Covers:

- Extended hardware coverage (up to 2 years or more)

- Two incidents of accidental damage coverage per year (subject to service fees)

- Battery service if your battery health drops below 80%

- 24/7 priority access to Apple experts

Cost of AppleCare+:

- Varies depending on Watch model and material.

- Usually billed annually or as a one-time upfront payment.

Is It Worth It?

- **Highly Recommended** if you are very active (running, sports, outdoor adventures) or simply want to avoid high repair costs for accidents like cracked screens.

- **Maybe Skip** if you are a very careful user, or plan to upgrade frequently (yearly).

Helpful Tip:

Even if you don't buy AppleCare+ immediately, you typically have **up to 60 days** after Watch purchase to add it (some regions allow longer windows).

Fact from Research:

Many real-world Watch users who have broken screens or experienced accidental water damage strongly recommend having AppleCare+, especially given the Series 10's higher repair costs compared to older models.

Chapter 12

Maintaining and Protecting Your Apple Watch

Cleaning and Caring for Your Watch

Regular cleaning not only keeps your Apple Watch looking its best but also ensures it functions properly—especially for sensors like heart rate and blood oxygen monitoring.

How to Clean Your Watch:

- **Turn off your Watch** and remove it from the charger.

- **Use a soft, lint-free cloth** (like a microfiber cloth) to wipe the Watch.

- **For heavier grime or sweat:**

- Lightly dampen the cloth with fresh water.

- Wipe the watch case, sensors, and band gently.

- Avoid using soaps, cleaning products, or abrasive materials.

Special Care for Bands:

- **Silicone and Sport Bands:**

  - Rinse under fresh water and dry with a soft cloth.

- **Leather Bands:**

  - Wipe with a dry cloth only. Avoid water—they are not water-resistant.

- **Metal Bands:**

- Wipe with a soft, slightly damp cloth, then dry immediately.

Helpful Tip:

Periodically clean the back of your Watch (where the sensors are) to maintain accurate heart rate, blood oxygen, and other health readings.

Fact from Research:

Users who clean their Watch weekly—especially after workouts—report better long-term sensor accuracy and maintain that "like-new" look longer.

Best Practices for Water Resistance

The Apple Watch Series 10 is built to handle water—but it's important to respect its limitations to maintain its water resistance over time.

What It Can Handle:

- Water resistance rating: **Up to 50 meters** under ISO standard 22810:2010.

- Safe for:

    o Swimming in pools and shallow open water

    o Wearing in the rain

    o Showering (though not with soapy or high-pressure water)

What to Avoid:

- Scuba diving

- High-velocity water (jet skiing, water skiing)

- Saunas or steam rooms (excessive heat and steam can damage seals)

Helpful Tips for Water Care:

- After exposure to saltwater or chlorine, rinse your Watch gently with fresh water.

- Activate **Water Lock Mode** before swimming to prevent accidental taps.

- After swimming, turn the Digital Crown to unlock and eject water from the speaker.

Important Reminder:

Water resistance is **not permanent**—it can diminish over time with normal wear or accidental drops.

Fact from Research:

Long-term users recommend avoiding

exposure to lotions, oils, or soaps directly on the Watch to prevent seal breakdown and water-resistance weakening.

Recommended Accessories (Bands, Screen Protectors, Chargers)

Adding the right accessories can extend the life of your Apple Watch and enhance your daily experience.

Bands:

- **Sport Bands:**
  Ideal for workouts, breathable and waterproof.

- **Leather Bands:**
  Great for casual or professional wear, but should be kept dry.

- **Solo Loop and Braided Solo Loop:** Stretchable, no-buckle options for maximum comfort.

- **Metal Bands:** Stylish for formal events; heavier but durable.

Screen Protectors:

- Highly recommended to guard against scratches and minor impacts.

- Options include:

  - **Tempered glass screen protectors:** High clarity and scratch resistance.

  - **Flexible film protectors:** Less noticeable, lighter protection for casual users.

Chargers:

- **Official Apple USB-C Magnetic Fast Charger:**
  Best for optimal fast-charging speeds.

- **Certified third-party stands:**
  Many offer elegant desk or bedside solutions, allowing you to see the Watch in Nightstand mode.

Helpful Tip:
Always buy **MFi-certified** accessories (Made for iPhone/Apple Watch) to avoid damage or poor performance.

Fact from Research:
Users who use screen protectors and protective bumpers on their Watch faces report significantly fewer scratches or cosmetic damage over time—especially for users who are active outdoors or in work environments.

Chapter 13

Final Mastering Tips

Little-Known Features to Try

Beyond the basics, your Apple Watch Series 10 hides several small but powerful features that can make everyday use even smoother and more enjoyable.

Walkie-Talkie App:

- Turn your Watch into a two-way communicator.

- Open the **Walkie-Talkie** app, invite a friend, and instantly send short voice messages with just a tap.

- Great for quick chats without typing or calling.

Smart Stack Widgets:

- Swipe up on the Watch Face (or use the Digital Crown) to access a Smart Stack of widgets.

- Displays relevant widgets throughout the day—calendar appointments, weather, workouts, reminders.

- Customize it by long-pressing and adding/removing widgets.

Backtrack Feature (Compass App):

- If you're hiking or exploring, the Watch can automatically track your path.

- Helps you retrace your steps if you get lost.

Tap to Pay Without Opening Apps:

- Simply double-click the Side Button, swipe to your desired card, and pay securely in seconds.

Silent Haptics for Alerts:

- You can enable "Haptic Alerts Only" for alarms and timers.

- Perfect if you want wake-up vibrations without disturbing your partner or coworkers.

Find Devices with Precision:

- Using the Find Devices app, you can locate your iPhone, AirPods, or even other family members' devices with precision tracking—especially useful when nearby but out of sight.

Helpful Tip:

Explore the **Settings → Accessibility**

section. There are hidden treasures like AssistiveTouch, VoiceOver, and larger text options that make daily use even more intuitive for every type of user.

Fact from Research:

Many users find the little features—like Walkie-Talkie, Smart Stack, and Find My Devices—become their "can't live without" functions once they start using them regularly.

Routine Maintenance for Peak Performance

A little bit of regular care ensures your Apple Watch Series 10 runs smoothly for years to come.

Software Updates:

- Always install WatchOS updates when available.

- Updates improve performance, patch security issues, and sometimes introduce new features.

Battery Health Monitoring:

- Check battery health every few months:

  Settings → Battery → Battery Health & Charging.

- If Maximum Capacity drops below 80% within warranty, battery replacement is covered by AppleCare+.

Cleaning and Care:

- Wipe down the Watch with a dry microfiber cloth weekly.

- Clean the bands—especially after workouts—to prevent sweat buildup.

- Rinse gently with fresh water after swimming or heavy exposure to dust.

Managing Storage:

- Offload apps you rarely use.

- Manage synced music, podcasts, and photos to free up space and keep the Watch fast.

Backup Regularly:

- Keep your iPhone backed up to iCloud or Finder (Mac).

- Your Apple Watch data is automatically included in the iPhone backup—this protects your settings, health data, and more.

Helpful Tip:

Set a calendar reminder to perform a "Watch Health Check" every three months—review battery health, free up storage, clean the Watch, and install updates.

Fact from Research:

Users who perform regular mini-maintenance routines report longer Watch lifespans, fewer software glitches, and more consistent battery life.

Appendix

List of Useful Settings to Explore

While you'll naturally discover many features over time, some settings can instantly improve your Apple Watch Series 10 experience if you know where to find them.

Display & Brightness:

- **Always-On Display:** Toggle to save battery or keep screen active.

- **Text Size and Bold Text:** Adjust for easier reading.

Sounds & Haptics:

- **Prominent Haptics:** Stronger wrist taps for important alerts.

- **Silent Mode:** Silences audible alerts while keeping vibrations active.

Battery:

- **Low Power Mode:** Enable to double battery life during long days.

- **Battery Health:** Monitor your battery's maximum capacity over time.

Accessibility:

- **AssistiveTouch:** Control the Watch with hand gestures.

- **VoiceOver:** Audio narration for screen content.

- **Zoom and Larger Text:** Easier viewing for those who prefer bigger fonts.

Workout Settings:

- **Auto-Pause for Workouts:** Automatically pauses your exercise tracking when you stop moving.

- **Power Saving Mode During Workouts:** Extends battery life by limiting heart rate monitoring.

Privacy Settings:

- **Health Data Sharing:** Choose what health and fitness data to share with apps or family members.

- **Location Services:** Customize which apps have access to your Watch's GPS.

Helpful Tip:

Spend some time exploring the **Settings** app directly on your Watch. Personalizing just a few options can dramatically improve your comfort and efficiency.

Common Apple Watch Symbols and Icons

Understanding Apple Watch icons helps you quickly interpret alerts and status information without confusion.

Symbol Meaning

Low Battery Warning

Connected to Wi-Fi

Do Not Disturb/Focus Mode is active

Sleep Focus Mode is active

Silent Mode is enabled

Symbol Meaning

💧	Water Lock is activated
⌚	Connected to iPhone
🔌	Charging in progress
▯	Connected to Cellular network
✳	Compass calibration needed or active
SOS	Emergency SOS call is in progress

Helpful Tip:

Swipe down from the Watch Face to check the Notification Center and see any important icons you may have missed.

Important Safety and Handling Information

Your Apple Watch is designed for everyday use, but it's important to treat it properly for maximum safety and longevity.

General Care:

- Avoid dropping, crushing, or exposing the Watch to extreme temperatures.

- Do not attempt to open or repair your Apple Watch yourself—only certified technicians should service it.

- Use only Apple-certified charging accessories.

Water Resistance:

- Water resistance isn't a permanent condition and can diminish over time.

- After swimming or heavy sweating, rinse the Watch with clean water and dry it thoroughly.

- Never charge your Watch while it's wet.

Health Features Disclaimer:

- Heart rate, blood oxygen, and sleep data are intended for general fitness and wellness purposes only.

- They are not medical-grade devices and should not be relied on for clinical diagnosis or emergency treatment.

Battery and Charging Safety:

- Stop using the Watch immediately if it becomes unusually hot.

- Do not expose the charging cable to liquids.

- Keep the magnetic charging cable away from very young children (small magnets can be dangerous if swallowed).

Helpful Tip:

You can always view the latest official Apple safety information by visiting Apple's website.

www.ingramcontent.com/pod-product-compliance
Lightning Source LLC
LaVergne TN
LVHW022349060326
832902LV00022B/4330